The Divine Setup: From Prison to Pulpit

"With great humility and thoughtful attention to detail, Shawn weaves a beautifully succinct and inspiring story of God's radical mercy and limitless grace. What transpires from *The Divine Setup* is a poignant reminder that none of us are too far from His great love. Having witnessed firsthand Shawn's journey throughout our fifteen-year friendship, I can attest that his willingness and absolute dependence on God has been the game changer. The result has been the hundreds of lives Shawn has impacted over the years—mine included."

—Blake Silverstrom
Nonprofit Executive Leadership

"The personal accounts of God's divine intervention in *The Divine Setup: From Prison to Pulpit* are heartwarming and soul stirring. I have personally witnessed the transformation in Shawn's life, and I am grateful that he has shared his trials and triumphs as a testament to what God will do when we surrender our hearts and lives to Him. This book is a great inspiration and a message that everyone should read."

—Cecilia Denmark, M.S.
Vice President and Chief Development Officer,
Bridges International

"Shawn O'Neil's *The Divine Set Up: From Prison to Pulpit*, is one of the most compelling stories of God's glorious redeeming power. Your life will be transformed as you read through the pages of his miraculous story, which all began with one person's answer of 'Yes!' to Jesus. All through Scripture and throughout generations, we see God knocking on the hearts of ordinary people to do an amazing work for Him. This is what Shawn O'Neil did years ago while sitting in a jail cell. Through his 'Yes!' an entire city and beyond have been impacted for Christ! This book will transform your life, compelling you to do more for God than you ever thought possible! Well worth the read!"

—Sol and Cindy Levy
Pastors,
New Life Church, Assembly of God (Dublin, CA)

"When I first met Shawn, I was a bit taken back, because he and a friend said, "What took you so long to get here? We have been praying for several months that you would be here to build strong knowledge of Scripture and help us and others to grow in our faith and new life in Christ." Shawn shared his guilt, shame, damage to others and himself—at which point we prayed together for God to forgive him and build a new life in Christ. At that point, it became evident that not only was he being transformed in his own life but sensed a call to teach and minister to others. When others said they wanted him to be part of what they were doing, I shared with him that he is charismatic and that many people urged him to join them. He chose to pray until he heard God's guidance, which he followed and continues to follow. His transformation has continued in faith, compassion for others, and in teaching and preaching the Word. I have been blessed to watch his Divine transformation, which this book accurately reflects."

—Ginery M. Twichell, M.Div., M.S., CAP, ICADC
Director of Chaplaincy,
Bridges International

"Oh, yes—the old things have passed away and the new has come! Blaise Pascal said, 'There is a God-shaped vacuum in the heart of every man which cannot be filled by any created thing, but only by God, the Creator, made known through Jesus.' Shawn's journey shows us that we only postpone our emptiness by trying to satisfy our thirst for life outside of Jesus Christ! When Shawn saw his need for mercy and experienced the abundant love of Jesus, he joyfully chose to live in glad surrender to Him. May we all do the same! Being forgiven sets us free! Shawn writes with such brave honesty—pointing us to Jesus Christ, the One who lifted him out of the miry clay and put him on a solid foundation with a new song in his heart! His journey shows us that the Lord Jesus is intimately seeking us and leading us to Him in the patchwork of our life's story. The heart of the reader will experience deep encouragement that life can move from regret to redemption, from pain to purpose and from shattered dreams to life-changing hope. Your heart will be captured by *The Divine Setup: From Prison to Pulpit.* There is no ruin beyond redemption. There are no bad choices made beyond the grace and transforming power of Jesus's love!"

—Dave Robinson
Executive Director of US Church Movements,
Cru®

"Step into the profound and inspiring journey of Shawn O'Neill as he unfolds the captivating narrative within *The Divine Setup*. Shawn fearlessly lays bare his tumultuous path—a journey marked by hardship, despair, and the unwavering presence of divine intervention.

In this compelling memoir, Shawn masterfully weaves together the threads of fate, choice, and faith, taking readers from the darkest depths of a prison cell to the radiant light of spiritual transformation. Every twist and turn in his story stands as a testament to the unmistakable presence of a God's power guiding his steps.

As you accompany Shawn through the highs and lows of his life, you will witness the incredible power of faith, the pursuit of redemption, and the unyielding guidance of a loving God. *The Divine Setup* serves as a poignant reminder that, even in our most desperate moments, God is at work, shaping our destinies in ways beyond our comprehension. All we must do is surrender to His call to follow Him.

This memoir transcends the genre—it is a testament to the intricate plan woven by a God who sees and knows all. Through its pages, readers will find solace, encouragement, and a renewed sense of hope, discovering that, no matter how challenging life may be, a divine setup awaits.

The Divine Setup is a powerful journey that speaks to the boundless grace of God and the transformative power of surrender. Shawn's story will deeply resonate with those who have struggled, despaired, or sought a deeper connection with the divine. I wholeheartedly endorse this book as a must-read for anyone in search of inspiration, encouragement, and a reaffirmation of faith in the face of life's greatest challenges."

—Pastor Thomas Manning
Senior Pastor, Christian Life Center

The Divine Setup: From Prison to Pulpit

Shawn Kelly O'Neill

Foreword by
Raeanne Hance

THE DIVINE SETUP: FROM PRISON TO PULPIT

Copyright © 2024 Shawn O'Neill. All rights reserved. Except for brief quotations in critical publications or reviews, no part of this book may be reproduced in any manner without prior written permission from the publisher.

ISBN 13: 979-8-218-96581-5

Cataloguing-in-Publication Data

The Divine Setup: From Prison to Pulpit by Shawn Kelly O'Neill; foreword by Raeanne Hance

xx + 100 p.; 23 cm. Includes bibliographical references.
ISBN 13: 979-8-218-96581-5
I. O'Neill, Shawn. II. Hance, Raeanne.
III. The Divine Setup: From Prison to Pulpit.

CALL NUMBER 2024

Manufactured in the U.S.A. 2024

Dedication

To Mom
You Know Why…

"Whoever is a believer in Christ is a new creation.
The old way of living has disappeared.
A new way of living has come into existence"
(2 Cor 5:17, GW).

Contents

Foreword

It is not every day that you get a front-row seat to watch a life being transformed.

The first time I met Shawn was at a gathering convened for returning citizens (ex-offenders) to collectively explore ways they could assist with the challenges they encounter upon reintegration into society. In that initial encounter, Shawn's uniqueness was unmistakable, and it became evident that an extraordinary plan was unfolding for his life. As circumstances aligned, Shawn joined the ministry where I served as the Regional Executive Director, and I assumed the role of his direct supervisor. It was during this time that I had a front-row seat to the unfolding chapters of Shawn's life.

Amid his search for purpose and the place the Lord had for him, Shawn's unwavering devotion to his Lord and Savior stood out as a constant. His love for his family mirrored this profound commitment, and it brings me immense joy to witness the remarkable trajectory the Lord has charted for him. I feel confident that this narrative only scratches the surface of the journey that lies ahead.

Knowing Shawn personally, I can affirm that his motivation for penning this book was not to bring glory to himself, but to write of the transformative power of the Lord Jesus Christ. Whether you find yourself grappling with life's complexities and questioning your purpose or simply seeking a source of encouragement, I wholeheartedly recommend reading *The Divine Setup: From Prison to Pulpit.* Shawn's story is not just his own—it is a testament to the resilience and redemptive power of faith, and you will find your own story enriched for having read it.

Thank you, Shawn, for baring your soul and allowing your story to be a blessing for so many. It is an honor and a privilege to write this Foreword, and I am so grateful for having had a part in the Lord's plan in your life.

—Raeanne Hance
Director of Global Community and Corrections | God Behind Bars
Ordained Minister - Gospel Crusade Ministerial Association

Preface

Life often takes us on unexpected journeys, weaving intricate tales that intertwine the threads of fate, choice, and faith. As I reflect on my own journey, I am struck by the undeniable presence of a Higher Power—a divine orchestrator who masterfully weaved every twist and turn into a tapestry of purpose and meaning. This is the story of *The Divine Setup.*

From the early chapters of my life, I found myself caught in the snares of circumstances that seemed destined to lead me down a path of despair and hopelessness. The shadows of poor choices and missteps cast a dark cloud over my existence, threatening to consume any glimmer of light. Yet, as the chapters unfolded, I came to realize that even in the depths of my struggles, God's hand was at work, setting the stage for a story that would defy all odds.

It was within the bleak confines of Broward County jail that I first began to understand the concept of divine intervention. Facing a potential ten-year prison sentence, my heart cried out for a second chance, a way to turn my life around. Little did I know that this cry would lead me to a spiritual crossroads—a place where my desperation met the outstretched hand of a loving God.

Through the iron bars of my prison cell, I discovered the power of prayer, the art of negotiation with the Divine, and the astounding reality of receiving an answer that held both relief and uncertainty. This was just the beginning of a series of events that would unfold with a precision that seemed almost scripted—each step marked by irony, redemption, and a profound sense of purpose.

As you delve into the pages of *The Divine Setup*, you will journey with me through the chapters of my life. From the quiet confines of my prison cell to the bustling streets of ministry, from the depths of addiction to the heights of transformation, you will witness the hand of God weaving a narrative that transcends human understanding.

This story is a testament to the interplay of free will and divine guidance, the dance between our choices and God's sovereign plan. This narrative speaks to the power of faith, the unyielding force of redemption, and the profound impact of a life surrendered to a greater purpose.

You will witness the hand of God weaving a narrative that transcends human understanding.

As the chapters unfold, you will encounter moments of despair, hope, struggle, and triumph. You will witness the intricacies of family, relationships, and ministry coming together in ways that only a divine orchestrator could author. Through every trial and victory, you will see how God's hand was at work—setting up divine appointments, creating opportunities for restoration, and leading me down a path that defies explanation.

Join me on this journey—one that unveils the divine setup that has shaped my life and that continues to unfold with each passing day. As you read, may you find encouragement, inspiration, and a renewed sense of awe in the intricate ways God weaves our stories into something far greater than we could ever imagine. *The Divine Setup* bears witness to the unfathomable depths of God's grace and the beauty of a life surrendered to His leading.

Acknowledgments

Melissa,

In the quiet moments of reflection, as I sit down to pen these words, I am overwhelmed by a deep sense of gratitude and admiration for the remarkable woman of God who has been the cornerstone of my journey—and specifically the journey of writing this book. Melissa, your unwavering support and selfless love have been my constant companions, giving me the courage and perseverance to see this project through to its completion.

Writing a book is often a solitary endeavor, one that demands hours of solitude and introspection. Yet, throughout this process, I have never felt alone, for you have been by my side, a steadfast presence that has offered comfort and strength in times of doubt and fatigue. Your belief in me, even when I questioned my own abilities, has been the driving force behind my determination to tell this story.

With all my love and gratitude,

Shawn

Vic,

Through all of life's twists and turns, you have been by my side, a constant presence on whom I can always rely. Whether it was the ups that we celebrated together or the downs that we faced with resilience, you've shown me the true meaning of brotherhood.

Beyond the pages of this book, our bond as brothers and friends is a treasure I hold close to my heart. I know that no matter what challenges lie ahead, I can always count on you to be there. This book is a small tribute to the friendship and brotherly love that has meant so much to me.

Kevin,

In the realm of inspiration and creativity, there's no one who has inspired me more than my middle brother, Kevin. Your passion for life and your boundless creativity have ignited a fire within me, and I want to express my heartfelt thanks for being such an incredible source of inspiration.

Greg,

To my baby brother, Greg, who has grown into an exceptional husband and father, I want to extend my heartfelt gratitude for the immense encouragement and inspiration you have been in my life. You've grown into a role model for me, showing me the importance of dedication, love, and the incredible joy that comes from building a loving family. This book carries a piece of the inspiration you've provided me.

Devin,

To my firstborn son, Devin, I want to convey my deepest gratitude and immense pride for the remarkable journey you have undertaken and the incredible odds you have overcome. You have not only made me proud as your father but have also been a profound source of inspiration and joy in my life. You are a mighty man of God. I love you, son.

Grace,

To my beloved daughter, Grace, who has always been the apple of her dad's eye, I want to express my deepest love and gratitude. You bring me immeasurable joy and inspiration. You are a strong, beautiful woman of God. I love you.

Noah,

To my beloved son and youngest child, Noah, your presence in my life brings me immeasurable joy and pride. Your heart for God and your infectious, energetic smile have been a constant source of inspiration. Your genuine love for God and the way you express it with such purity have taught me valuable lessons about the importance of faith and spirituality. You are a mighty warrior for God. I love you Noah J.

Chapter 1

Seeds of an Unfolding Tale: The Early Years (Origin Story)

The seeds of my story were planted amid the vibrant and transformative 1960s, in a world brimming with change and the promise of new horizons. My parents, emblematic of their time, were products of the blue-collar heart of middle America. They navigated the currents of those dynamic years, striving to make their mark on a world undergoing a remarkable evolution.

My mother and father, embodiments of the dreams and aspirations of their generation, set out on their journey together against the backdrop of a shifting landscape. The 1960s were a tumultuous era, marked by social upheaval, political unrest, and an undeniable spirit of rebellion. It was a time of transformation and transition, when traditional norms were challenged, and new paths were forged.

As children of their environment, my parents embraced the values and aspirations prevalent during those years. They believed in hard work, in the idea that they could build a better future through sweat, dedication, and a dash of the American dream. They were woven into the fabric of their community, living lives that echoed the chorus of a nation in flux.

The blue-collar ethos that defined their upbringing provided the crucible that shaped their characters. The values of determination, resilience, and loyalty were etched into their very beings. They knew the meaning of an honest day's work and the satisfaction that comes from standing on the foundation of one's own labor.

The 1960s were also a time of aspiration, when the world seemed to expand at an unprecedented rate. The space race captivated imaginations, while civil rights struggles and anti-war protests sparked conversations that echoed from the streets to the halls of power. Within this tapestry of social transformation my parents, like countless others, sought to find their place and purpose.

As I trace the threads of my own story back to these formative years, I am reminded that every life is a patchwork of experiences, influences, and choices. My parents' journey through the 1960s laid the groundwork for my own path, intertwining with the larger narrative of history. Their struggles and triumphs, dreams and disappointments, all became integral threads in the tapestry of my existence.

In the chapters that follow, I delve deeper into the tale of my origins, exploring the impact of my parents' lives on mine, and how the echoes of those years reverberate through the grand narrative still unfolding. Just as their story was shaped by the era in which they lived, so too was mine shaped by their choices, their values, and the world they helped shape. And so, with an eye on the past and a heart toward the future, let us embark on this journey through time and experience the remarkable tapestry of life that is *The Divine Setup.*

Chapter 2

Conceived in the Shadows/ From Darkness to Light

The story of my existence, like many tales, began with a blend of light and shadow, joy and sorrow. It was 1973, a time when the echoes of the sixties still reverberated through the culture, and society was grappling with the complexities of changing norms. I was conceived in a world of shifting boundaries, where the line between tradition and rebellion was blurred.

My parents, caught between the tides of their era, found themselves in a situation that tested the boundaries of social convention. Conceived outside the bounds of wedlock, my entry into this world carried with it the weight of secrecy and societal judgment. As the child of an unconventional beginning, my life would forever be shaped by the choice my parents had made.

Just as my story was beginning, tragedy cast its shadow over our family. In January of 1974, a month before my birth, my grandfather's life was abruptly extinguished. While crossing the street to his own house, he was struck by a hit and run driver and left for dead. His departure left a void that would be deeply felt, even by a newborn who would never have the chance to know him. The fragility of life and the swift currents of fate were etched into my earliest memories, a reminder that every step we take is a dance with destiny.

On a chilly February day in 1974, in the city of Detroit, I entered a world marked by contradictions, making my debut into a reality filled with paradoxes. Born out of wedlock, I carried with me the whispers of societal disapproval that clung to my existence. The circumstances of my birth, a testament to the complexity of human relationships, would set the tone for the narrative unfolding.

As the years rolled on, my family's story evolved in unpredictable ways. In 1976, my mother took a step toward stability by marrying the man who would become my stepfather. However, the sanctuary of family life remained elusive as the shadows of alcoholism and abuse loomed large over our home. My childhood was tainted by the scars of anger and fear, leaving me yearning for a sense of belonging that always seemed just out of reach.

Amid the turmoil, my love for baseball emerged as a constant, a refuge where I could find solace and a sense of control. The baseball diamond provided a space where I could momentarily set aside life's uncertainties, allowing me to pursue dreams with the same passion that others sought in their escapes from reality.

In 1977, the first glimmer of an extended family appeared with the birth of my brother, Vic. However, the challenges persisted as the cycle of pain and dysfunction continued. The tapestry of my upbringing was woven from a blend of experiences—some filled with joy, some tainted by sorrow—but always infused with a longing for the family I had yet to find.

From an early age, I became acquainted with the haunting presence of death and grief. In 1985, my world darkened with the loss of my brother, Mikey, diagnosed with leukemia when he was very young. Despite our hopeful wishes, his time on this side of eternity was tragically brief. He left us at the tender age of five, serving as a stark reminder that life, as precious as it is, can be incredibly fleeting. The pain of his absence deeply etched into my soul a profound awareness of mortality..

Life in the Motor City wasn't easy, and the tough exterior I developed was a survival mechanism. I found myself getting tangled up with drugs and gangs, desperately seeking a way out of the harsh realities that surrounded me. Little did I know that these choices were leading me down a path that limited my opportunities and boxed me into a corner.

Navigating the rough seas of adolescence, I managed to graduate from high school in 1992. The following year, seeking a new direction and a fresh start, I enlisted in the U.S. Army. It was a pivotal decision that would thrust me into a world of discipline, structure, and camaraderie—a stark contrast to the tumultuous life I had known.

At the age of twenty-one, my life was ensnared in a whirlwind of reckless choices and shattered dreams. The pivotal moment came on the night of a tragic accident that not only saw me lose control of the car but also resulted in the loss of my stepdad, a significant figure in my life. The weight of grief and remorse pressed down on me, propelling me further into a downward spiral of alcohol-fueled chaos. The details of that evening haunted me for years. Earlier, my parents and I had visited a local establishment, a bar my stepdad frequented during his years of employment at Detroit Diesel. He was in pain, and I convinced him to smoke a joint to alleviate it. When caught by the bar manager, they demanded we leave immediately. My mom stayed behind, and I left with the intention of returning later. Upon reaching home, I found my dad asking for my mom, and in his impaired state, we decided to go back to the bar. During the drive in our new Nissan Sentra, my dad encouraged me to accelerate. As we sped through a green light, the rain started, causing the car to hydroplane. The loss of control led to a collision with a tree, resulting in the car splitting in half. Shocked and disoriented, I woke up in one half of the car while my stepdad was in the other. Emergency responders later confirmed his death at the scene, leaving me in disbelief.

Amid my darkest moments, the Divine intervened again, extending a hand to spare my life once more. This instance was not merely about avoiding a tragedy on the road but about confronting the repercussions of my choices. Looming prison gates posed a threat, ready to confine me for the pain I had inflicted. I found myself charged with DUI manslaughter.

Even during my darkest moments,
the hand of the Divine reached out
to spare my life once more …
intervening once again, steering
me away from a path
of destruction.

However, a miracle transpired. The doors that were supposed to close behind me stayed open. In that bewildering and astonishing moment, the burden of my family's grief and my own guilt weighed heavily on me. It became clear that this was beyond my comprehension, far more than mere coincidence. Despite the justifiable expectation of a fifteen-year prison sentence, by the grace and mercy of God—though I did not recognize it then—I was spared, and the judge granted me probation.

This unexpected twist of fate struck my family like a thunderbolt. My brothers, Victor, Kevin, and Greg were already grappling with the loss of our dad, and now they were confronted with the possibility of losing me to the justice system. I was adrift, lost in the sea of my own poor choices, searching for a lifeline to hold onto.

Little did I know that the lifeline given to me was being woven by the Divine. It wasn't just luck or chance that kept me from those prison walls; it was the intricate design of a Higher Power working in ways I couldn't comprehend. As I look back on that pivotal moment, I see the hand of God intervening once again, steering me away from a path of destruction.

As I share this chapter of my journey, I'm reminded that even in the depths of our mistakes and the pain we've caused, there's a greater plan at play. The divine setup was in motion, and I was being led to a place where I could find healing, redemption, and purpose.

Now, as I reflect on the journey that brought me to today, I cannot help but wonder how the pieces of my life have fit together, how each twist and turn has shaped the person I've become. The chapters that have unfolded so far have carried me through a landscape of trials and tribulations; yet, as I set my sights on the horizon, a glimmer of hope beckons—a hope that the story is far from over, that redemption and transformation still have their place on this winding path.

Chapter 3

Dance with the Devil: 2002 Hollywood, FL (Selling Ecstasy to Undercover Police)

Life has a way of leading us down paths we never anticipated, sometimes guided by our own choices, and sometimes pushed by circumstances beyond our control. As I reflect on my journey, one incident stands out—a moment that would prove to be a pivotal turning point, a clash between desperation and the allure of quick riches. This is the story of the day I danced with the devil in Hollywood, Florida.

The year was 2002, and I found myself in a place of uncertainty, grappling with the need to make ends meet. The weight of responsibility pressed heavily on my shoulders, and I was willing to explore avenues I never imagined just to find a way out of the darkness that seemed to perpetually linger.

Hollywood, Florida—a name that conjures images of glitz and glamour—held within its shadows a different reality, one where desperation and ambition collided. It was here I was introduced to a risky hustle, a shot at making fast cash by pushing ecstasy—an illicit substance that dangled the prospect of financial relief, yet carried the threat of dire repercussions.

The plan, though intricate in its simplicity, revolved around my connection to a network guaranteeing a constant flow of ecstasy pills. The temptation of quick money was irresistible, akin to a siren's song luring me into perilous waters. Disregarding the cautious whispers of reason, I succumbed to the allure, enticed by the chance to break free from the burdens of financial hardship..

The dealings were clandestine, the exchanges shrouded in secrecy. Each transaction sent my heart racing, a mixture of adrenaline and fear coursing through my veins. Every interaction was a tightrope walk between survival and self-destruction, a gamble with stakes higher than I had ever known.

As the days turned into weeks, I found myself entangled in a dangerous dance with the devil. The thrill of the illicit trade was intoxicating, masking the underlying dread that gnawed at my conscience. I became skilled at navigating the underground world, learning the art of disguise and deception to stay one step ahead of the law.

But in the underbelly of Hollywood, nothing remains hidden forever. As fate would have it, the line between reality and performance blurred when I unknowingly sold ecstasy to an undercover police officer. In an instant, the stage I had been performing on crumbled beneath me, replaced by the cold, harsh reality of arrest.

The road ahead was uncertain, but amid the darkness, a glimmer of clarity emerged.

Handcuffed and exposed, I confronted the consequences of my decisions. The pursuit of ill-gotten gain had guided me down a perilous road, and now I teetered on the edge of legal repercussions that loomed, ready to dismantle any semblance of the future I had imagined.

As I look back on that moment—a pivotal scene in my life's narrative—I see the threads of desperation and vulnerability woven into the tapestry of my decisions. The dance with the devil had revealed its true face, and the consequences were inescapable. It was a wake-up call, a stark reminder that shortcuts and easy money come at a cost—one that can irreversibly alter the course of one's life.

As I stood there in the aftermath of my choices, I began to grasp the complexity of the divine setup—the intricate interplay of circumstance, choice, and consequence that had brought me to this juncture. The road ahead was uncertain, but amid the darkness, a glimmer of clarity emerged—a realization that the next chapter of my life would be defined not by the mistakes of the past, but by the choices I made moving forward.

Chapter 4

Echoes of Redemption: In the Joseph Conte Facility: A Divine Response to Desperation

The Joseph Conte Facility in Broward County was a place where time seemed to stand still, where the weight of our mistakes bore down upon us, and where the ironic twists of fate played out in the most unexpected ways. Here the convergence of my hopes, fears, and the unforgiving reality of my choices would bring me face to face with a kind of salvation I could never have anticipated.

I found myself thrust into this cold, harsh world, my future hanging in the balance as I faced the specter of a ten-year prison sentence for my involvement in MDMA trafficking. The allure of easy money and a misguided sense of invincibility had led me down a treacherous path. Now, as I sat alone in a two-man cell, the consequences of my actions crashing down around me, I felt an overwhelming sense of despair.

The irony of it all was not lost on me. In a world where I had yearned for a family, for emotional support and the promise of something lasting, my choices had shattered those dreams. A marriage that had barely begun was now strained by the weight of my actions, and the words that cut through the phone line only served to deepen my desolation.

"I can offer you nothing more than a friendship, and there's no way in hell that I will ever bring our child into prison," she had said. The woman who had been my partner for years, the one I had dreamed of building a life with, now stood at a crossroads that didn't include me. The hope that had been my lifeline was now gone, replaced by an abyss of isolation and regret.

In the solitude of that cell, as darkness enveloped me, I found myself crying out, my voice a raw and desperate plea: "God, please help me, because I have ruined my life!" The words echoed off the cold walls, a raw admission of defeat, yearning for and yielding to something greater than myself to intervene.

Then, in the stillness that followed, I felt Jesus—His presence, a response that seemed to cut through the darkness and reach into the depths of my heart and soul. In a moment that defied explanation, I heard a whisper—a voice that seemed to come from within and beyond, declaring with a certainty that sent shivers down my spine: "I'm here with you. Son, you're going to be OK."

"I'm here with you. Son,
you're going to be OK."

It was an answer that carried a weight of its own, an answer that held both promise and uncertainty. In a world of chaos and consequences, here was a whisper that seemed to transcend the boundaries of reality. Had I truly heard Jesus, the Divine? Could this be a glimpse of redemption, a sign that there was still hope for a future beyond these prison walls?

As the legal proceedings unfolded, negotiations took place, and plea deals were offered, that whisper remained with me—a constant companion in a world of uncertainty. Then, in a final twist of irony, the gavel fell, and the sentence was pronounced: five years. The cosmic negotiation, the plea that had been both desperation and faith, had been answered in a way that I could never have anticipated.

In that moment, I realized that salvation could emerge from the most unlikely of places, that even within the confines of a prison, Jesus can reach through and offer a glimmer of hope. The journey ahead would be long and the challenges formidable, but within that whisper I heard a reminder that I was not alone.

As the days turned into years, I held onto the irony that, in a place of darkness, I had found a connection to something greater, something that defied the limitations of my circumstances and whispered of a second chance. Jesus had saved me!

Chapter 5

Divine Call: From Fasting to Prophecy (A Journey to Lead in God's Army)

In the heart of my spiritual journey, a chapter unfolded that would forever alter my understanding of purpose and destiny. It was a chapter steeped in faith, marked by fasting, and crowned with a divine prophecy that would set me on a path I could have never imagined.

Following my transformative experience at the Joseph Conte Facility, a fire was ignited within me—a determination to answer a higher calling, make amends for my past, and bring light to the lives lost in the shadows. Yet, while wrestling with the weight of this profound calling, I yearned for validation and a sign, especially considering I was still incarcerated at this point in my journey. I sought assurance that I was genuinely on the right path.

In my quest for confirmation about what direction my life should take, I turned to a period of fasting and prayer. Days turned into nights, and I sought solace in the presence of God, longing for guidance and reassurance. During this time of profound devotion the idea of being a general in God's army began to take shape in my mind—an idea both audacious and humbling.

Nonetheless, a quiet voice within me whispered that this was not merely a product of my own desires but a divine whisper, a call to something greater. And so, with unwavering conviction, I embarked on a journey that would lead me to the doorstep of a prophet—a vessel through whom God's voice would be heard.

I vividly recall the day I stood before the prophet, heart pounding and hope burning brightly within me. As he laid his hands upon me, a surge of energy coursed through my being—a sensation that transcended the physical realm. Then, as if the barriers between heaven and earth had momentarily dissolved, the prophet began to speak:

"Son," his voice carried the weight of ages, "I see you on a mountain ridge, a commander in God's army. You will lead a battalion of tanks, symbols of strength and power. Yes, you are a general in God's army."

Tears welled in my eyes as his words washed over me. It was a moment of profound revelation—a confirmation of the call that had been echoing in my heart. But the prophecy did not end there. The prophet's voice grew even stronger, resonating with an authority that left no room for doubt.

"You will be a beacon of light in dark and dangerous places," he declared, his voice unwavering. "You will lead the liberation of many who have been cast away, discarded by society. Through your ministry, lives will be transformed, and the power of God will be made manifest."

"You will be a beacon of light in dark and dangerous places," he declared.

In that moment, I felt a merging of the earthly and the divine—a connection that transcended time and space. The prophet's words were not just a declaration but a commission—a charge to embrace a destiny set in motion long before I ever took my first breath.

As I reflect on that transformative chapter of my life—the chapter that began with fasting and culminated in a prophecy—I am struck by the irony of my journey. From a life marked by choices that led me down a destructive path, I had emerged as a chosen vessel—a vessel to carry hope, healing, and redemption into the lives of those who had been marginalized and forgotten.

The weight of the prophet's words would stay with me, guiding me through the challenges that lay ahead. With each step, I would strive to embody the role of a general in God's army, leading with courage, compassion, and an unwavering belief in the transformative power of divine grace. As I looked to the future, I knew that the mountain ridge was not just a destination but a symbol of the heights to which faith and purpose could carry me.

From that day forward, I carried the prophet's words with me—a mantle of responsibility and purpose. The journey that lay ahead was one filled with challenges and triumphs, with moments of doubt and moments of unwavering faith. But through it all, the vision of leading a battalion of tanks on a mountain ridge remained etched in my mind—a symbol of the calling I had received, a calling that would lead me to places I had never imagined and impact lives in ways I could have never foreseen.

The rise of a general had begun—an ascent fueled by prayer, prophecy, and a resolute belief in the extraordinary. As I stepped onto this path, I knew that my life was no longer my own; it was a vessel for something greater—for the power and mercy of the Divine.

Chapter 6

Divine Relocation: Unfolding of God's Plan

Life is often a complex interplay of choices and circumstances, where our journey takes unexpected turns and twists. Yet, sometimes, there's an unmistakable sense that a Higher Power is orchestrating these intricate threads, weaving them into a tapestry of purpose. My journey had been anything but ordinary, and as I stood on the threshold of my next chapter, I felt the profound hand of the Divine moving in ways I could never have foreseen.

After the transformative encounter with the prophet and the powerful vision of leading a battalion of tanks, I found myself facing another chapter of divine intervention—a chapter that involved a geographical shift of profound significance.

As I prepared to leave the prison facility in the panhandle of Florida, I could not help but marvel at the chain of events that had led me there. It was a place close to my family, a place where the support and connection with loved ones had provided solace during my time of incarceration. Yet, as I boarded the metaphorical train of destiny once again, I knew that this journey held a deeper purpose.

Lawtey, Florida, near Jacksonville, became my new temporary home. At first, things seemed surprisingly good. The atmosphere felt more conducive to growth and change, and the proximity to my family brought a sense of comfort. It was as if God's hand had led me to this place, providing me with an environment that seemed ripe for transformation.

But as life has taught me, the divine plan is often mysterious and far-reaching, its design unfolding gradually, like a story gently revealing its plot. Just as I settled into a rhythm in Lawtey Correctional Institution, feeling a sense of stability and purpose, the wheels of fate began to turn once again.

One day, as I walked along with my fellow inmates, heading to the chow hall, a prison officer's voice cut through the air with an unexpected announcement, "Son … You're going to Pompano Beach!"

Pompano Beach—a city only thirty minutes away from my son, where I would be closer to him than I had ever been during my time of incarceration. It was a revelation that struck me with the force of destiny itself. In that moment, I realized the profound implications of this transfer. God had not only moved me from twelve hours away from my son to only thirty minutes away, but He had done so with such precision that it felt impossible to ignore the divine hand at play.

Jesus was directing my path with a purpose that transcended the confines of my current reality.

The journey from the panhandle to Lawtey had been a preamble, a steppingstone to the true purpose of my relocation. God had guided me, orchestrated circumstances, and paved the way for me to be close to my son. It was a reminder that even in the darkest of moments, even in the confines of prison, there is a grander plan at work—one that defies human logic and exceeds human understanding.

As I stood on the precipice of this new chapter, I could not help but feel awe-struck by the ways in which God's plan was unfurling before my eyes. The intricate dance of events, the alignment of circumstances, and the unmistakable sense of divine intervention all pointed to a truth that had become irrefutable in my journey: I was not alone in this struggle, and the hand of a Higher Power was guiding me. Jesus was directing my path with a purpose that transcended the confines of my current reality.

With a heart full of gratitude and a renewed sense of purpose, I embraced the next leg of my journey—a journey that would take me to Pompano Beach, a journey that held the promise of a deeper connection with my son and a journey that continued to illuminate the extraordinary power of a plan far greater than my own.

Chapter 7

Divine Whispers: Echoes of Grace and Revelation

Spring 2006 brought with it an air of renewal and a sense of hope and transformation that seemed to mirror the state of my own heart. I found myself sitting alongside a quiet trail, surrounded by the vibrant hues of nature in full bloom. The sun's gentle warmth kissed my skin, and a soft breeze carried the fragrance of new beginnings.

As I took in the beauty around me, I closed my eyes and allowed the tranquility of the moment to wash over me. It was in this serene setting that I heard it—a voice that resonated not only within my ears, but deep within the core of my being: "When I was on the Cross, I was thinking of you."

The words were simple, yet they carried a weight that transcended their apparent meaning. They spoke of a love so profound, a sacrifice so immense, that it was almost overwhelming to comprehend. It was as if the Divine was whispering directly to my soul, reminding me of the unwavering connection between us.

In that instant, I felt a surge of emotion—a mixture of gratitude, humility, and a renewed sense of purpose. The realization that I was the subject of such divine contemplation filled me with a profound sense of significance. It was a message of affirmation, a reassurance that I was never alone on this journey, no matter how challenging it became.

The words echoed in my mind as I walked back to my quarters, a sense of awe accompanying every step. Hours later, as the day transitioned into evening, I found myself drawn to the chapel for prayer and Bible study—a space that had become a sanctuary of solace and revelation.

Upon entering the chapel, I was met with a sight that left me speechless. There, hanging on the wall of the chaplain's office, was a new cross—one that had not been there before. Its message mirrored the very words I had heard earlier that day: "When I was on the Cross, I was thinking of you."

"When I was on the Cross,
I was thinking of you."

I stood there, gazing at the Cross in awe, my heart pounding with a mixture of disbelief and wonder. It was as if the Divine had orchestrated a visual representation of the message I had received earlier—a confirmation that the words were not mere figments of my imagination, but a true and profound communication from a higher source.

Tears welled up in my eyes as I contemplated the intricacies of this divine encounter. The synchronicity of the message, the timing of its delivery, and the tangible representation of those words—all of it testified to the mysterious ways in which God communicates with us, the intricate dance of signs and whispers that guide us on our path.

From that day forward, the message became a guiding light in my life—a reminder of the boundless love that had been extended to me, a love that transcended my past mistakes and encompassed the entirety of my being. That love fueled my determination to continue seeking spiritual growth, to share the message of redemption with others, and to live a life that reflected the transformative power of grace.

As I walked away from the chapel that evening, my heart was filled with a profound sense of gratitude. The voice of God had reached me amid nature's splendor, and its resonance had echoed through the walls of a humble chapel. It was a reminder that divine whispers are all around us, if only we have the ears to hear and the heart to receive.

Chapter 8

Whispers of Release: Divine Promises and Unexpected Turns

The pages of my journal have always been a sanctuary—a place where my thoughts could flow freely, unburdened by the constraints of reality. It was within these pages that I often found solace and, at times, a profound connection with the Divine. Little did I know that one journal entry would become a conduit for a message that would both guide and challenge me.

As I sat down to write, pen in hand, the words seemed to spill forth effortlessly. I found myself pouring out my hopes, my fears, and my yearnings for the future. Then, during my reflections, I felt a presence—a whisper that seemed to come from within and yet beyond me. "When you are released, you will be with your family."

The words hung in the air like a promise, a declaration of a future that held the potential for reconciliation, unity, and the restoration of what had been lost. I knew, with a certainty that transcended explanation, that this was a message from God himself. It was a pledge that ignited a spark of hope within me, a light that would guide me through the remainder of my time behind bars.

Armed with this divine assurance, I embarked on a journey—a journey that would ultimately lead me to pursue the mother of my son. Although our relationship had been fractured by circumstances and choices, I believed that the promise I had received was a harbinger of change, a testament to the redemptive power of God's grace.

Something profound clearly had shifted within her as well. I could sense a softening, a recognition of the importance of a father's presence in a child's life. She too had been touched by the Divine, and together, we began to navigate a path toward healing and reconciliation. It wasn't an easy road, and there were moments of doubt and uncertainty, but the promise I held in my heart fueled my determination.

Miraculously, she agreed that our son deserved the love, guidance, and influence of both his parents. This, in itself, was a testament to the transformative power of God's touch—a power that could mend even the most broken of relationships. We began to envision a future where we could co-parent, where our son would know the unity of his parents, and where love would triumph over past hurts.

But then, in a moment that blindsided me, she looked into my eyes with a mixture of sadness and resolve and said, "You have to move on with your life." Her words cut through the air with a weight that left me stunned. "I am not the one for you."

The contradiction between her words and the promise I had received was jarring. How could the divine assurance I had held so dear clash so starkly with her declaration? It was a moment of turmoil, a collision of hope and reality that left me grappling for understanding.

Yet, in my confusion, I realized that the promise I had received wasn't a guarantee of a specific outcome but rather an assurance of divine presence and guidance. It was a promise that had led me to take the steps I needed to heal and reconcile, and in that sense, it had already been fulfilled.

The journey had taught me that God's promises were not always about controlling circumstances, but about shaping hearts and leading us toward growth and transformation. As I navigated the complex emotions of that moment, I held onto the knowledge that God's plans often unfold in ways we can't anticipate, and His wisdom surpasses our understanding.

God's promises were not always about controlling circumstances, but about shaping hearts and leading us toward growth and transformation.

The whisper in my journal had set me on a course of restoration, and while the outcome wasn't what I had expected, I knew that God's hand was still guiding me, shaping me, and teaching me to trust in His unfailing love—even when the path was fraught with unexpected turns.

Chapter 9

Promises Fulfilled: Divine Words of Reassurance

Life has a way of weaving intricate patterns, threads of destiny and chance that intersect in ways we can only begin to comprehend. As I walked this journey of redemption and restoration, I found myself standing at a crossroads of doubt and hope, wrestling with the promise I had received, and the unexpected turns life had taken.

Amid the uncertainty, a new chapter began to unfold—one that carried the potential to reshape not only my story, but also the story of the young life that had been entwined with mine. It was a chapter born from the depths of divine assurance, a promise that had echoed in my heart even in the face of contradictory circumstances.

I recall a moment of clarity, a moment when a prophetic voice spoke words that would illuminate the path ahead. "Your absence will not harm your son. In fact, it will be as if you never left. Your relationship will flourish, and you will experience a bond that transcends time lost." The words were a balm to my soul, a beacon of light amid lingering doubts.

As I clung to those words, I realized that this promise was not just about a future relationship with my son; it was a testament to the boundless grace and mercy of a God who could restore what had been broken. It was an affirmation that the tapestry of our lives was being rewoven, and the threads of separation were being replaced with threads of connection, love, and understanding.

Over time, as the barriers between us began to crumble, I witnessed the truth of the promise unfolding. It was as if the years of absence were being erased, replaced by shared moments, laughter, and the kind of companionship I had yearned for. Our relationship grew, not hindered by the past, but enriched by the present.

"Your relationship will flourish,
and you will experience a bond
that transcends time lost."

Together, we embarked on a journey of discovery—one that allowed us to learn about each other anew. Through conversations, shared interests, and the simple joy of spending time together, I saw the truth of the prophetic words coming to life. The chasm created by absence was closing, and a bridge of connection was forming, strong and unshakable.

As we navigated life's challenges and celebrated its victories, the promise continued to resonate in my heart. I marveled at the beauty of divine restoration, the way God's hand could mend what had been torn and bring healing to wounds that had long festered. Through it all, I was reminded that God's timing was far more perfect than I could have imagined.

The story that unfolded was not just one of a father's return but a story of two hearts finding their way back to each other. It was a story of grace upon grace, of second chances and new beginnings. As I looked into my son's eyes, I realized that the promise wasn't just about me but about the legacy of love and redemption we were building together.

In the end, the words spoken in that prophetic moment held true. The absence, pain, and years lost were no match for the power of a God who could mend, restore, and transform. Our relationship flourished, just as it had been foretold, and I knew that the journey of restoration was far from over. It was a journey that had led me to a place of profound gratitude, a place where I could bear witness to the miraculous workings of a God who truly makes all things new.

Chapter 10

Serendipity and Slices of Fate: Love's Entrancing Arrival

Life is a labyrinth of twists and turns, each bend leading to unexpected destinations. As my journey through redemption and restoration continued, I found myself at a crossroads once again, a juncture where the divine orchestration of events became strikingly evident.

The day seemed routine, or so I believed, while I continued to navigate it within the constraints of work release. I was engrossed in my work, crafting sandwiches with care and precision, relishing the simple joy that came from creating something delicious. Little did I know that the wheels of destiny were turning, propelling me toward an encounter that would forever change the course of my life.

Without warning, the veil of familiarity was torn asunder. The job I had come to rely on, the means by which I could contribute to my reintegration into society, was snatched from my grasp. I was fired, not for anything I had done but for reasons beyond my control. In that moment, confusion and fear set in. It was as if the ground beneath me had given way, leaving me suspended in a state of uncertainty.

Returning to my work release dorm that evening, a whirlwind of emotions raged within me. Anxiety gnawed at my heart as I grappled with the apparent setback. Yet, during the storm, I turned to the only source of solace I knew. I prostrated myself on the cold floor, offering up a simple prayer to the heavens above: "God, you know these prison administrators; I am in work release, they want their money. I need a job. Amen."

As I rose from my place of supplication and exited the room, a divine twist of fate unfolded before me. Another inmate approached, bearing a piece of paper with a number inscribed upon it. A number that led to a pizzeria just down the street—where they were in search of a pizza maker. The coincidence was too palpable to ignore, and I rushed to the phone to make the call.

The voice on the other end belonged to the owner of the pizzeria, and he invited me for an interview. Swiftly, I found myself standing in the bustling pizzeria, the aroma of fresh dough and melting cheese enveloping me. It was there, amid the hum of ovens and the clatter of utensils, that the threads of destiny wove together in an unforeseen pattern.

Hired on the spot, I stepped into my role at the pizzeria. The routine of crafting pizzas became a dance, a rhythm that echoed the beat of my renewed hope. Yet, it wasn't until the third day—a day like any other—that the scene shifted, and a new character entered the narrative of my life.

In walked a vision, a beautiful young lady who seemed to radiate a glow that transcended the ordinary. Our eyes met, and in that instant, time seemed to stand still. It was as if the universe had conspired to bring us together, orchestrating a serendipitous meeting that defied explanation.

Her name was Melissa, and from the moment our gazes intertwined, I knew that something extraordinary was unfolding. It wasn't just attraction—it was a recognition, a deep-seated knowing that our paths were meant to cross. Love, they say, can be a slow-burning ember, but in this instance, it was a blazing fire that consumed my heart.

As the days turned into weeks, I discovered that Melissa shared my passion for creating culinary masterpieces. We talked, laughed, and shared stories, as if we were two pieces of a puzzle finally finding our place in the grand design. Our conversations flowed effortlessly, carrying with them the promise of a connection that was as profound as it was unforeseen.

Our conversations flowed effortlessly, carrying with them the promise of a connection that was as profound as it was unforeseen.

Looking back, it's astonishing to consider how a single prayer, a simple request for a job, set into motion a chain of events that led me to that pizzeria. And it was within those very walls that destiny unveiled its most precious gift—a love that had been written in the stars, a love that would shape the chapters yet to come. Amid broken roads and unexpected turns, the serendipity of that encounter was a testament to a divine plan that far exceeded my wildest dreams.

Chapter 11

Reunion of Hearts: Freedom (A Journey Home)

April 7, 2007, marked a day that had etched itself into my heart four years prior, when I first entered the somber realm of the Florida Department of Corrections. But on this day, the sun shone a little brighter, and the air felt crisper as the weight of those years began to lift. As I walked out of the prison gates on that long-awaited day, I was met with a sense of liberation unlike any other.

Waiting for me was Melissa, my partner in life, a woman who had stood by me through the darkest days of my journey. Her embrace was a testament to the enduring power of love and commitment, a bond that had weathered the storms of separation. With her by my side, I felt a renewed sense of purpose, a determination to make the most of the fresh start that lay ahead.

Even in the darkest of times, there is a thread of hope that weaves its way through our lives.

Our first stop was her parents' home, a brief visit filled with warm smiles, hugs, and a shared sense of hope for the future. From there, the journey continued to my brother's house in Delray Beach—a place that held the promise of family and connection. And there, an extraordinary gift awaited me.

Erika, the mother of my son, Devin, had already ensured that our reunion would be one of joy and unity. She had entrusted Devin into the loving care of his Uncle Victor and Aunt Jen, a gesture that spoke volumes about the transformation that had taken place within our relationships. Being an integral part of my son's daily life after four long years was an immeasurable gift, a testament to the miraculous power of healing and forgiveness.

But the story didn't end there. As our family gathered in the car, anticipation filled the air as we embarked on a journey to Jacksonville. It was a journey of both miles and emotions, a pilgrimage to reunite with the heartbeats that had been a source of strength throughout my life. In Jacksonville, my mother, brothers, grandmother, aunts, uncles, and cousins awaited, their presence a reminder of the ties that bound us together.

As we came together under the same roof, the atmosphere was charged with a mixture of laughter, tears, and a sense of unity that transcended the trials we had faced. I looked around at the faces that had seen me through my darkest days, and I marveled at the realization that this was exactly as God had spoken. The divine promise had been fulfilled in ways that were beyond my comprehension at the time of its utterance.

The reunion was more than just a gathering; it was a testament to the power of faith, resilience, and the unwavering support of family.

The reunion was more than just a gathering; it was a testament to the power of faith, resilience, and the unwavering support of family. As we shared stories, caught up on life's events, and simply reveled in each other's presence, I felt a deep sense of gratitude. The journey that had begun with mistakes and consequences had led me to this place of redemption and restoration.

As the day concluded and I looked around at the faces of those I held dear, I knew that I had been given a second chance—not just at freedom, but at life itself. The promise had been fulfilled, and it was a reminder that even in the darkest of times, there is a thread of hope that weaves its way through our lives. On that day, in the embrace of family, I found myself at the intersection of past, present, and future—a place where the divine setup had led me to a place of grace.

Chapter 12

A New Beginning

Embracing Redemption

Stepping into the light of my newfound freedom, a fresh chapter of life unfolded—a chapter resonating with the hope of a God-centered existence, marital commitment, the prospect of children, and the anticipation of unknown adventures. The past, a crucible of lessons, gave way to a present filled with the promise of renewal and the complexities of living in the vibrant landscape of South Florida.

With the freedom to embrace this new journey, the freshness of walking with God became a guiding light amid the uncertainties of the path ahead. In the complexities of South Florida living, Melissa and I stood on the precipice of the unknown, ready to explore the uncharted territories that awaited us.

On December 7, 2007, against the backdrop of the holiday season's magic, Melissa and I exchanged vows in a ceremony that blended the celebration of love with a profound testament to the power of second chances. The bond forged through trials and triumphs was officially sealed, marking our commitment to navigate the complexities of life hand in hand, embracing the mysteries and adventures that lay ahead.

Restoration: Divine Appointments and Unexpected Encounters

As we settled into our life together, the threads of destiny continued to weave a tapestry of events that would shape our journey. Our path led us to the anticipation of a new life—a life that would soon be blessed by the arrival of our daughter. With this anticipation came the preparation for a baby shower, an event that would set the stage for one of the most unexpected divine appointments.

The Marie Green Forum for Global Missions had repeatedly caught our attention through a radio ad urging people to host their events at The Forum. It was as if the universe itself was guiding us toward this place. And so, in obedience to what felt like a divine nudge, we reached out to them to host our baby shower. Little did we know that this decision would serve as a catalyst for something much greater.

In an uncanny twist of fate, our connection with The Forum led me to David Hoskins. A chance meeting scheduled with him at Malulo's Peruvian restaurant in Pompano turned out to be the beginning of a remarkable journey. As we sat together over lunch, conversation flowed, stories were shared, and it became evident that this encounter was not coincidental.

David Hoskins was not just anyone—he was the son of a general in the army of God, Bob Hoskins. The founder of Book of Hope International ministries (now called OneHope), Bob was a man of great influence and purpose. Through David our lives intersected with the legacy of faith that the Hoskins family embodied.

Chapter 13

Divine Encounters: A Confluence of Purpose

As I sat across from David Hoskins, I felt the weight of destiny hanging in the air. Our paths had converged in a way that defied explanation, and it was clear that something greater than ourselves was at work. David's demeanor exuded a sense of purpose and conviction, and it didn't take long for our conversation to reveal the depth of his faith and the mission that drove him.

Over the course of our lunch, David shared about his family's journey in founding Book of Hope—an organization committed to reaching the next generation with the message of the gospel. The stories he shared painted a vivid picture of lives transformed and hope restored. It was as if the essence of our own journey of redemption was mirrored in the work of Book of Hope.

> I saw the threads of destiny weaving once again—a tapestry that connected my past to my present, my mistakes to my redemption, and my pain to my purpose.

Then, as if guided by a force beyond our understanding, David extended an invitation—one that held the potential to reshape my path once again. He spoke of a job opportunity within Book of

Hope, an opportunity that felt like a convergence of my own journey and the divine call to impact lives. As he extended the offer, it was as if the universe itself held its breath, waiting for my response.

In that moment, I realized that this was not just a job offer but an invitation to participate in a movement that aligned with my own journey of restoration. It was a chance to serve as a vessel of hope for those who had lost their way, just as I had once lost mine. The irony of it all—how the divine setup had led me to this crossroads of purpose and service—was not lost on me.

And so, as I considered David's offer, I saw the threads of destiny weaving once again—a tapestry that connected my past to my present, my mistakes to my redemption, and my pain to my purpose. In the journey that had led me from the darkness of a prison cell to the light of hope, I realized that the divine setup was not just a series of coincidences, but a divine orchestration that had guided me to this very moment.

Chapter 14

Testimony of Transformation: Unveiling Redemption

In the quiet hum of the office, amid emails and the steady rhythm of work, an unexpected message arrived one morning. It was an email from Blake Silverstrom, Director of North America for OneHope, the organization that had become the beacon of purpose in my life. The email announced the weekly staff chapel and extended an invitation to share personal testimonies—a chance to stand before my colleagues and share how Jesus saved me.

A rush of excitement coursed through me as I read the email. This was an opportunity to open up about my journey, to unveil the redemption story that had transformed my life from its darkest depths to the light of hope. Without hesitation, I replied, stating that I indeed had a testimony to share, and I eagerly accepted the invitation to speak at the upcoming staff chapel.

As the days passed and Wednesday drew near, a sense of anticipation settled within me. The weight of the story I was about to share was significant, and I felt a mix of nervousness and determination. Outside of the founder and his family, no one at OneHope knew about my past—my history of drug dealing and reckless behavior. To them, I likely appeared to be a model Christian, far removed from the turmoil of my earlier life.

When the day of the staff chapel finally arrived, I stood before a room filled with my colleagues—individuals who had dedicated their lives to spreading hope and faith. They were, by all appearances, the embodiment of piety and righteousness, and I couldn't help but feel like an outsider among them. As I began to share my story, their attentive eyes widened in surprise.

The story of my past unfolded—the drug trafficking, the darkness, the desperation. I spoke about the turning point, the moment of surrender that had led me to God's embrace. I shared how the journey of redemption had not only transformed me but also led me to a purpose-driven life through OneHope. The irony of it all was not lost on anyone—the transformation that had taken place within me was a testament to the power of God's grace.

As I spoke, I saw expressions of shock, awe, and ultimately, a sense of realization in the eyes of my colleagues. They had known me as the man who had found salvation, but they had not known the depths from which I had emerged. The contrast between my past and present self was a vivid reminder of the redemptive power of faith.

They had known me as the man who had found salvation, but they had not known the depths from which I had emerged.

In the wake of my testimony, there was a tangible shift in the atmosphere. The room seemed to buzz with a renewed sense of purpose and inspiration. I could sense that my story had resonated with my colleagues, reminding them that transformation was possible for anyone willing to embrace it.

From that point forward, my role within OneHope took on a new dimension. I was entrusted with the opportunity to work on creating a new B*ook of Hope for inmates*—a project that held personal significance and aligned with my own journey. Through the grace of

God, my redemption story had become a source of inspiration for others and a reminder that no one is beyond the reach of hope and transformation.

Chapter 15

A Divine Appointment in Prison Ministry: Answering the Call to Serve

As I continued my journey with OneHope, I couldn't help but feel amazed by the way God orchestrated each step of my redemption story. The influence and impact I was gaining within the OneHope community were only the beginning of a much greater plan—one that would lead me to an even wider platform for service.

In a twist that only God could engineer, my path converged with one of the most renowned prison ministries in the world—Chuck Colson's Prison Fellowship. Through a series of providential events, I found myself receiving an invitation to join their team as a reentry field director in Florida. This was a monumental step, a door flung wide open by divine intervention.

As I stepped into my new role, I felt a deep sense of purpose and responsibility. Chuck Colson's legacy of transforming lives behind bars resonated deeply with me, and I was honored to participate in this mission. The work of Prison Fellowship was far-reaching, and I knew that my own journey of transformation had uniquely prepared me to play a role in the lives of those seeking a second chance.

On my first day at Prison Fellowship, I was met with a remarkable experience that felt like a page taken out of Joseph's story in Egypt. I arrived at Everglades Correctional Institution with a mix of excitement and anticipation. Little did I know that I was about to encounter a display of unexpected favor.

As I entered the facility, I was met by the warden, the assistant warden, and even the Colonel himself. This was an unusual reception, as high-ranking officials seldom took the time to personally greet a new staff member. I was taken aback by their warm welcome and their eagerness to show hospitality.

To my surprise, they led me to a room where a sumptuous feast awaited. The warden, assistant warden, and Colonel insisted on serving me an elaborate meal, treating me like an honored guest. I had never encountered such an act of generosity and kindness like that before, and I couldn't help but draw parallels to Joseph's time in Egypt when he was elevated to a position of influence.

In that moment, I felt the presence of God's favor surrounding me. It was as if God was confirming His hand on my journey, reminding me that He was orchestrating every step. This divine appointment with the prison officials served as a powerful affirmation of my purpose in the realm of prison ministry.

In that moment, I felt the presence of God's favor surrounding me.

As I settled into my role at Prison Fellowship, I embraced the opportunity to impact lives and advocate for those reentering society after incarceration. My own story of redemption became a bridge of connection, allowing me to speak from a place of understanding and compassion. It was a privilege to walk alongside individuals navigating the challenges of reintegration, offering them hope and guidance on their journey to transformation.

The path that had led me to Prison Fellowship was a testament to the divine setup that had been unfolding in my life. The influence I had gained within the prison ministry community, coupled with the opportunities that arose, affirmed that God's hand was at work. I was stepping into a new chapter—one where my redemption story was interwoven with the stories of countless others seeking a fresh start.

Chapter 16

Kingdom Connections and Unforeseen Journeys: Guided by Divine Appointments

In the intricate tapestry of our lives, the threads of destiny are often woven by connections that transcend our understanding. As I continued my journey within the realm of prison ministry, I encountered a series of remarkable individuals—Kingdom emissaries who played pivotal roles in shaping my path.

One such emissary was Raeanne Hance, the Executive Director of Prison Fellowship in Florida. Raeanne invited me to Christian Life Center in Fort Lauderdale, Florida, where Prison Fellowship's mentoring program would be shared during the World Mission's convention on a Wednesday evening. Little did I know that this seemingly routine event would usher me into a series of divine encounters that would change the trajectory of my life.

It was at Christian Life Center that I had the privilege of meeting Pastor Max and Ophelia Yeary. This meeting proved to be a catalyst for a profound mentoring relationship that would become a cornerstone of my spiritual journey. Pastor Max took me under his wing, offering guidance, wisdom, and a profound connection that went beyond the surface. Through his mentorship, I was able to glean from his experience and insight, allowing me to grow both as a servant of God and as a leader within the ministry.

Under Pastor Max's guidance, I embarked on a path that led to the fulfillment of a lifelong dream—one intricately connected to my transformation. Through his encouragement and support I pursued my credential as a certified minister with the Assemblies of God. This milestone marked a new chapter in my life, affirming the ways in which God was using my redemption story to empower and equip others.

Little did I know that this seemingly routine event would usher me into a series of divine encounters that would change the trajectory of my life.

During this season, another calling emerged—one that resonated deeply with my own journey. Together with a group of fellow ex-offenders, we birthed a ministry that catered to individuals transitioning from prison to society, as well as their families. Our shared experiences allowed us to create a space of understanding and support, providing a lifeline for those navigating the challenges of reintegration.

As our ministry took root and flourished, unforeseen circumstances tested our faith and commitment. One of our newest members suffered a heart attack, sending shockwaves through our tight-knit community. In a show of solidarity, we gathered at the hospital, ready to offer our prayers and support. It was in the lobby of that hospital that yet another divine connection was unveiled.

Sol and Cindy Levy, the Outreach Pastors of Christian Life Center, crossed our path that day. Their presence was no accident; it was a divine orchestration. Little did I know that this encounter would bear significant fruit in the years to come. Their kindness, empathy, and heart for outreach resonated with the mission that had been laid on my heart.

Years later, Pastor Sol shared a revelation that left me astounded. He confided, "The day I met you, God told me you would be the Outreach Pastor of CLC." That revelation was a testament to the intricate ways in which God had been weaving our paths together, aligning our visions and purposes for greater Kingdom impact.

In the grand tapestry of my journey, these interconnected moments formed a constellation of divine appointments. Kingdom emissaries—like Raeanne Hance, Pastor Max and Ophelia Yeary, Pastor Sol and Cindy Levy—served as guides, mentors, and collaborators on a journey that continued to unfold with purpose and promise.

Chapter 17

Culinary Dreams and Redemption Ventures: From Culinary School to Culinary Ministry

In the annals of my life's journey, an unexpected chapter unfolded—one that intertwined my passion for culinary arts with my unwavering commitment to ministry. It was a chapter that saw the birth of New Creations Catering, Miry Clay Ministries, and an endeavor that would bridge the gap between culinary arts and rehabilitation within the walls of prisons.

Even amid the challenges of life, I found myself making a decision that would significantly alter my trajectory prior to my incarceration—I enrolled in culinary school. Those two years spent pursuing an associate degree in culinary arts were transformative. My skills flourished, and a once distant passion for cooking became an integral part of my identity. I often humorously mused that before Jesus, my first passion was cooking, and I even entertained notions of becoming "the Christian Bobby Flay," igniting the world with my culinary creations.

Yet, life had other plans. The responsibilities of raising a family on a ministry salary prompted me to innovate. Thus, New Creations Catering was born, with its foundation rooted in 2 Corinthians 5:17—a verse that declares, "Therefore, if anyone is in Christ, the new creation has come: The old has gone, the new is here!" This venture not only offered delectable cuisine but also embodied the transformative power of redemption, exemplifying the newness of life that Christ brings.

As New Creations Catering gained momentum, a larger vision began to take shape—one driven by a calling to bring culinary arts and hope into prisons. The idea was simple yet profound: to provide culinary training programs within the prison walls, offering inmates an alternative path and the chance to develop marketable skills. Undergirded by mentorship and support, this initiative aimed to empower those incarcerated with practical tools for their future.

The idea was simple yet profound: to provide culinary training programs within the prison walls, offering inmates an alternative path and the chance to develop marketable skills.

Simultaneously, Miry Clay Ministries was formed—a vessel through which we could extend mentorship and in-prison ministry. Our hearts resonated with those who found themselves in the depths of despair, much like I once had. We recognized that true transformation required more than just a change of location; it necessitated an inward renewal of identity and purpose that only Jesus could bring.

One of the significant milestones during this period was our engagement with Bridges of America, an organization that bridges the gap between incarceration and community re-entry, specifically with the Bridges of Pompano Beach work release facility. Having graduated from this program, I held a special connection with its mission. Under the leadership of Director Cecelia Denmark and Chaplain Ginery Twitchell, I found great favor and an open door to engage with those on their own journey of restoration.

Invited back as a speaker and mentor, I felt humbled to have the opportunity to share my story and faith with the men behind those walls. Miry Clay Ministries facilitated in-prison mentoring sessions that aimed to break chains and ignite hope. Additionally, New Creations Catering brought a touch of culinary excellence, providing not just food but a reminder of the new creations we were all becoming in Christ.

Between 2009-2012, the seeds of my endeavors took root. I co-founded the non-profit organization, Out of the Miry Clay, a testament to the transformative power of redemption. Simultaneously, New Creations Catering continued to flourish, bridging the gap between culinary artistry and ministry. These ventures embodied my belief that God's redemption reaches even the darkest corners, bringing forth beauty from the ashes.

As I reflect on this chapter of my journey, I am reminded that God's plan is never limited by our circumstances. Through the union of culinary arts and ministry, I witnessed lives transformed, stories rewritten, and hope rekindled—a testament to the boundless possibilities that unfold when we align our passions with God's purpose.

Chapter 18

Unveiling a New Season: Embracing New Leadership and Educational Pursuits

The pages of life's narrative turned swiftly, and as the dawn of 2012 graced the calendar, so did a new era for Christian Life Center in Fort Lauderdale. The reins of leadership shifted from the capable hands of Pastor Max to the dynamic duo of Tom and Candi Manning, a missionary couple who had overseen an international church in Vienna, Austria. The anticipation was palpable, and I found myself caught up in the currents of change.

I had the distinct privilege of meeting Pastor Tom, the newly appointed lead pastor, for a breakfast conversation. The air was charged with excitement as we sat across the table discussing the potential this new season held. At that point, my aspirations were aimed at achieving the next level of ministerial credentials within the Assemblies of God—a pursuit that reflected my ever-deepening commitment to the call of God on my life.

Pastor Tom's encouraging words resonated with me as he urged me to connect with Pastor Steven Chapman, another member of the Christian Life Center staff. This remarkable young individual had recently graduated with double masters from Gordon Conwell Theological Seminary. It was suggested that I inquire about the new Southeastern University program and explore how I could become a part of it. Eager to seize the opportunities unfolding before me, I took Pastor Tom's advice to heart and reached out to Pastor Steven.

Before long, the wheels were set in motion. What began as a conversation with Pastor Tom and a prompt from Pastor Steven led me on a journey that took me from aspirations to reality. I found myself seated within the confines of a boardroom at Christian Life Center, my heart racing with anticipation. There, I learned that I was being granted the incredible opportunity to enroll as a full-time student at Southeastern University—a pursuit that would see me working toward a Bachelor of Science in Ministerial Leadership.

The tapestry of my life seemed to be woven with divine threads, each encounter and conversation leading me closer to the purpose that God had intricately designed for me. From a life marked by desperation and despair, I had journeyed through redemption and restoration, only to find myself embraced by a community that saw beyond my past and believed in my potential. Pastor Tom's vision for the future mirrored the transformation that God had worked within me, igniting a fire of hope that burned brighter with each passing day.

Each encounter and conversation led me closer to the purpose God had intricately designed for me.

As I embarked on this new educational chapter, I did so with a heart full of gratitude and a determination to make the most of the opportunities before me. The winds of change were sweeping through Christian Life Center, and I felt humbled to be a part of a congregation that embraced growth, innovation, and a relentless pursuit of God's purpose. Little did I know that this was just the beginning of a journey that would see me further equipped, empowered, and positioned to impact lives in ways I could have never imagined.

Chapter 19

Convergence of Dreams: When Passions Unite (A Divine Appointment)

As the sun cast its golden rays upon the horizon, the day I had been eagerly awaiting finally arrived—a day that marked the convergence of two worlds that had once seemed separate yet were now intertwining in ways only God could orchestrate.

With the dawn of that new day, I found myself preparing for my very first class as a student at Southeastern University, an institution deeply rooted within the legacy of Christian Life Center. I was filled with anticipation as I contemplated the journey ahead, the knowledge waiting to be gleaned, and the growth sure to unfold in the hallowed halls of academia. Little did I know that what was happening in the background would soon thrust me into a role that would amplify my impact in ways I had never imagined.

While engrossed in my academic preparations, a divine encounter was unfolding behind the scenes—a rendezvous that held the promise of shaping the path ahead. Through my nonprofit work with Bridges of America, I had crossed paths with Dr. Thomas Beckner, the chaplain supervisor for the organization's corporate office in Orlando. An invitation for breakfast led me to the table of destiny, a table where conversations shifted from the ordinary to the extraordinary.

As I savored the meal before me, the conversation took an unexpected turn, opening a door I hadn't even realized was standing in front of me. What had begun as a potential expansion of our mentoring sessions into other Bridges of America facilities quickly evolved into a proposition that left me both elated and astonished. Dr. Beckner spoke of a role within Bridges of America—one that aligned perfectly with my heart's deepest passions.

He unveiled an opportunity that felt like a dream come true: the role of Transitional Housing Director for Bridges of America. This role would place me at the helm of a program that provided housing for men transitioning out of prison, a program that had the potential to bring hope, transformation, and new beginnings to those seeking to rebuild their lives. This was a promise of thirty-six beds for thirty-six lives that could find restoration, redemption, and reintegration into society.

The application process was set in motion, and my heart raced with anticipation as I navigated the steps toward this new opportunity. Yet, amid the excitement, unexpected opposition emerged. The Department of Corrections questioned the wisdom of hiring me, given the compensation contract that Bridges of America had with them. However, God's hand was evident in every twist and turn of this journey. Lori Constantino Brown, president of Bridges of America, journeyed to Tallahassee to advocate for my candidacy, highlighting the transformative impact I could have on the lives of those transitioning from prison.

As I embarked on my way to my first class at Southeastern, my heart carried a sense of expectancy. Before parting ways with Dr. Beckner, we decided to grab lunch to further discuss the unfolding developments. In that moment, with the phone call Dr. Beckner received, my dreams and destiny collided. With joy in his eyes, he proclaimed, "Welcome aboard! You got the job!"

As those words resonated, I couldn't help but marvel at the divine choreography at play. With the weight of this amazing opportunity now resting on my shoulders, I drove toward my first class at Southeastern University as the newly appointed Director of Transitional Housing for Bridges of America. The convergence of passions and the alignment of purpose—all stood in front of me as a testament to the divine setup that had woven itself intricately into the fabric of my life.

Chapter 20

An Unfolding Path: Divine Progression (From Restoring Lives to Leading Souls)

As my journey at Southeastern University continued, so did the remarkable transformation within the transitional housing program I had undertaken. Stepping into my role as the director, I encountered a challenging reality—only three residents occupied the space, each grappling with their own battles. Nevertheless, I was armed with a divine template—a plan of action birthed from the whispers of the Lord himself. It was a blueprint for bringing structure, purpose, and healing into the lives of these men.

The journey was not without its challenges, but with the encouragement of the corporate office and my direct supervisor, I had the freedom to implement the changes necessary to usher in the results we all hoped for. I dove headfirst into the work—conducting phone interviews, attending reentry fairs, and conducting intake evaluations that provided a holistic understanding of each resident's journey. I helped the residents find jobs, secure clothing, and navigate the complexities of reentering society.

Amid this endeavor, a twist of fate brought me to a rendezvous with Professor Steven Chapman; a conversation over donuts at Krispy Kreme would alter the course of my life once again. He extended a proposal—an opportunity to join the staff at Christian Life Center. Stunned and unsure of how to proceed, I turned to my supervisor,

Ginery, with a plea for guidance. "Chap, the church has offered me a job. I don't know what to do. Will you please pray for me?"

As I continued to labor at the transitional house, the seeds of transformation began to sprout. The once-desolate space was now nearly full, bustling with life and renewed hope. The impact was undeniable. Structure was replacing chaos, restoration was overtaking brokenness, and the promise of a future untainted by drugs and crime beckoned. My yearning to make a difference was manifesting before my eyes.

My yearning to make a difference was manifesting before my eyes.

Amid the blossoming progress, spring 2013 arrived, marking the completion of my first full year of college courses. It wasn't just academic growth that I was experiencing, though, but spiritual revelation. The voice of the Holy Spirit spoke with clarity, guiding me toward a new path. "Go to Christian Life Center. The leadership development you will receive is what is needed for the next step." With this divine affirmation, I took the leap of faith. I tendered a two-month notice to my supervisor and began the transition.

June marked the commencement of a new season, one where I embraced the role of a candidate to take over the transitional housing program. As my journey within the transitional house came to a close, I was embarking on a new chapter—one where my calling to restore lives and lead souls would converge, intertwining my passion for ministry, mentorship, and transformation.

With the knowledge gained at Southeastern University and the guidance of the Holy Spirit, I entered a phase of my life that held the promise of equipping me for what lay ahead. The challenges I had faced, the lives I had touched, and the divine appointments that had marked my path—all were threads weaving together a narrative that was guided by a higher purpose—one that would continue to unfold with every step I took on this journey of restoration and divine calling.

Chapter 21

A Tapestry of Family and Ministry: Uniting Hearts, Vision, and Divine Calling

The tapestry of our journey had been intricately woven with threads of family, faith, and divine appointments. As I looked around, my heart swelled with gratitude for the life that had unfolded before me, shaped by both the trials we had overcome and the blessings that had poured down upon us.

It was a moment of celebration—Melissa and I were marking five years of marriage, cherishing the life we had built together. Our family had grown to include two precious children, Grace and Noah, who brought joy and purpose into our lives. As we stood on the threshold of another milestone, the reality of our eldest son, Devin, entering middle school, brought a mixture of nostalgia and anticipation.

Five years earlier, our hopes had been buoyed by the prospect of Devin coming to live with us. In that pivotal conversation with Erica, Devin's mother, Melissa and I had expressed our desire to provide Devin with a home grounded in faith and love. Although we had left that meeting with high expectations, reality had dealt us a different hand—the email that followed from Erica outlined her reasons for not allowing him to live with us.

Fast-forward five years, and here we were again, facing the prospect of Devin coming to live with us as he entered middle school. The excitement was palpable, the vision of a restored family providing the driving force behind our actions. Despite the obstacles that had arisen before, we embraced this opportunity with hope, seeing it as a culmination of our prayers and dreams.

During this transformative time, new doors were opening within the ministry at Christian Life Center. Positions that resonated with my passions and skill set were presenting themselves, offering a chance to serve and make an impact. The opportunity to join the outreach ministry and work alongside Pastor Sol, my predecessor, was an honor. Our collaborative efforts bore fruit, expanding the reach and influence of the church's outreach.

Despite the obstacles that had arisen before, we embraced this opportunity with hope, seeing it as a culmination of our prayers and dreams.

Yet, as the church's vision evolved toward a multi-site strategy, another door swung open—one that would shift my journey yet again. An invitation to the launch team, and lead community outreach for Christian Life Center's first campus in Coral Springs emerged, offering growth, challenge, and an avenue to further serve the community. With our hearts attuned to God's guiding whispers, we accepted the task.

The Coral Springs campus launched in September 2015, and our family embraced this new chapter with enthusiasm. Saturday nights found us united in worship, joining the Coral Springs congregation in their faith journey. It was a year marked by growth, as both our family and the campus flourished.

Amid this season of change and expansion, another milestone beckoned—my graduation from Southeastern University in the spring of 2016. With high honors, I received my bachelor's degree in ministerial leadership, a testament to the transformation and growth I had experienced on this journey.

Amid these developments, the culmination of divine orchestrations was unfolding. Pastor Tom extended a remarkable offer—a position as the Outreach Pastor at Christian Life Center. The realization that this role encompassed the very essence of my passion and calling was undeniable. My heart swelled with gratitude as I considered the path that had led me to this point.

As I reflect on these moments of transition, I'm reminded that every step, every challenge, and every triumph was part of God's intricate design. Our family and ministry were united by His divine hand, intertwined in a narrative that spoke of restoration, purpose, and unwavering faith. With Devin's presence in our home, the expansion of our ministry, and a heart full of gratitude, I stepped into this new role, eager to see the continued work of the divine setup unfold.

Chapter 22

Filling Big Shoes: Embracing a Divine Mandate to Step into a Legacy of Outreach

The mantle of outreach had been passed on to me—one that carried with it a legacy of impact and service. As I stepped into the role, I couldn't help but feel the weight of the shoes I was about to fill. The shoes were indeed large, filled by those who had come before me, leaving indelible footprints on our community and beyond.

The responsibility was both humbling and exhilarating. The path ahead was paved by those who had tirelessly sought to bring hope, compassion, and transformation to the lives of others. It was a legacy built on the foundation of Christ's love—a foundation that I was now entrusted with upholding and expanding.

The shoes I was stepping into were not just physical but symbolic of a commitment to the call of service. They represented countless hours spent on the streets, in shelters, and in the hearts of the hurting. They embodied the prayers lifted for broken, lost, and marginalized people. They signified a willingness to go where others might not venture, to embrace the uncomfortable, and to shine a light in the darkest corners.

As I contemplated the journey ahead, I couldn't help but reflect on the stories of transformation I had witnessed throughout my own life. From prison cells to pulpits, I had experienced firsthand the power of God's grace to redeem and restore. Now, as I stepped into this role, I felt compelled to share that same message of hope with a world that desperately needed it.

As I embarked on this new phase of ministry, though, I remained keenly aware of the challenges that lay ahead. The shoes I was filling weren't just big; they had been worn by giants who had navigated the intricacies of outreach with grace and dedication. It was a daunting prospect—to continue the work they had begun, to build upon their foundation, and to carry forward a torch that had burned brightly for years.

Yet, amid my apprehension, I found strength in the knowledge that I was not alone on this journey. The support of my family, my church community, and above all, God's guidance, provided me with the assurance that I was called and equipped for the task at hand. As I stood at the crossroads of past and present, I understood that the shoes I was filling were a symbol of continuity—a reminder that God's work was ongoing and that I was merely a vessel through which His love would flow.

The shoes I was filling were a symbol of continuity—a reminder that God's work was ongoing and that I was merely a vessel through which His love would flow.

The shoes may have been big, but they were also a reminder that this was not a journey to be embarked upon in my own strength. I was following in the footsteps of those who had gone before, leaning on their wisdom and experience as I navigated the challenges of outreach. More importantly, I was following in the footsteps of Christ, who had shown me what true compassion, love, and service looked like.

As I stepped forward, my heart filled with both determination and reverence. I was embracing a divine mandate, a call to carry the legacy of outreach and impact forward, to touch lives, and to bring about transformation. With each step I took, I was reminded that the shoes I was filling were not just shoes—they were a symbol of God's faithfulness, His provision, and His unwavering commitment to His people. As I walked in those footsteps, I knew that the journey ahead was one filled with purpose, grace, and the undeniable presence of the divine setup.

Chapter 23

Divine Shifts and Appointments: Unexpected Turns and Providential Encounters

Life's trajectory is often a series of unpredictable turns, and the night that Pastor Nadine Raphael's call came was no exception. Little did I know that this seemingly ordinary phone call would set in motion a new chapter in my journey. The conversation revolved around my education and the prospect of pursuing a master's degree. At that moment, the idea felt both reasonable and exciting, and I agreed to embark on a two-year master's program in ministerial leadership with Southeastern University.

As the fall semester of 2019 commenced, my anticipation for this new academic pursuit grew. The first few months of classes were promising, and everyone was looking forward to the mid-winter break. However, no one could have predicted what was on the horizon—the global lockdown that would define the year 2020.

Through the uncertainty that the pandemic brought, an opportunity emerged in February 2020. I was presented with the chance to attend a conference in Orlando called Exponential. Little did I know that this conference would be a catalyst for a divine appointment that would shape my understanding of evangelism and ministry.

Prior to attending Exponential, I had wrestled with a significant question—how could we shift our approach to evangelism from a confrontational style to one rooted in relationships and friendship?

The statistics and insights from Barna's "Reviving Evangelism" study weighed heavily on my heart, revealing that traditional confrontational methods often turned people away.

During this time of prayer and contemplation I found myself at the "Changing the Face of Evangelism" pre-conference workshop at Exponential. The hosts, David Robinson, Gabor Gresz, and Amy Karst from Cru Church Movements became instrumental figures in shaping my perspective. As the workshop unfolded, I realized that the answer to my question lay in building authentic relationships and engaging in meaningful conversations rather than simply presenting a gospel message.

How could we shift our approach to evangelism from a confrontational style to one rooted in relationships and friendship?

The convergence of my quest for a new approach to evangelism with the insights from the workshop was nothing short of providential. I saw how God's hand had orchestrated the timing and the encounters, bringing me to this place of revelation. As I interacted with David, Gabor, and Amy, I felt a resonance with their vision and their heart for reaching people in a relational way. Their experience and wisdom were invaluable, and I knew that this encounter was a divine appointment.

Little did I know that this newfound understanding of evangelism would permeate the next phase of my ministry journey. The master's program continued amid the challenges of the pandemic, and my perspective on outreach, discipleship, and ministry was shifting. As the world grappled with uncertainty, I felt a renewed sense of purpose—a call to embody the love of Christ through authentic relationships, genuine conversations, and intentional discipleship.

Looking back, it's clear that this chapter of my journey was marked by divine orchestration. From the call that led me to pursue a master's degree to the encounter at the Exponential conference, God was aligning the pieces of the puzzle. He was guiding me toward a ministry approach that resonated with His heart—a journey both humbling and empowering.

As the world grappled with uncertainty, I felt a renewed sense of purpose—a call to embody the love of Christ through authentic relationships, genuine conversations, and intentional discipleship.

As I stood on the precipice of this new understanding, I felt filled with a sense of awe and gratitude. God had brought me to a place where my passions, experiences, and calling converged—a place where I could continue to serve Him in ways that honored His heart for people. The path ahead was still uncertain, but I knew that I was walking in step with the divine setup, embracing the shifts and appointments that were shaping my life and ministry.

Chapter 24

The Unforgettable Ordination: Unshaken by Global Challenges

September 20, 2020, will forever stand as a testament to the unwavering plans and purposes of an Almighty God—a date etched into my memory as the day of my ordination as a minister of the gospel. It was a milestone that the global pandemic could not deter, for the call of God is unshakeable, regardless of circumstances.

The anticipation leading up to my ordination was brimming with a sense of reverence and honor. Typically, such a sacred event would take place during the yearly district council of the Assemblies of God. However, complications brought about by COVID-19 had shifted the course of events. Nevertheless, permission was granted to hold the ordination service on our church campus—a divine arrangement that held a profound significance for me.

As the day approached, a mixture of excitement and humility welled up within me. The one who would officiate my ordination was none other than my senior pastor, Dr. Thomas Manning—a man of deep wisdom with a heart for God. To be ordained within the walls of Christian Life Center, my spiritual home, added an extra layer of significance to the occasion. And in a world that had been temporarily reshaped by the pandemic, the live streaming of the event meant that friends and family from far and wide could share in this pivotal moment of my faith journey.

September 20, 2020, dawned as a day bathed in both anticipation and significance. Before God and a congregation that had become like family, with Melissa by my side, I stood ready to make a solemn covenant to love and serve the Lord with all I am and to extend that love and service to my neighbors as myself. It was a moment of profound commitment, one that resonated not only with those present but with the unseen realms as well.

Guided by Pastor Tom's words, I accepted the weighty mantle that comes with ordination. His charge was a clarion call to step boldly into the path set before me, to preach, teach, and proclaim the Word of God without compromise. The charge was not just a list of instructions but a divine commission that demanded a steadfast heart and a commitment to unwavering truth. The responsibilities were significant, but they were woven together by the thread of a singular purpose: to serve the Lord and His people wholeheartedly.

I was stepping into a sacred calling.

The ceremony held moments of both solemnity and celebration. The laying on of hands by Pastor Tom symbolized a spiritual transference—a recognition by the body of Christ that I was set apart for a unique role. As he spoke the words of ordination, I felt a deep sense of gratitude and purpose wash over me. I was stepping into a sacred calling that stretched beyond human accolades and recognition.

Now, as I reflect upon that day, I'm reminded that being on the stage and in the pulpit is not about the desire for prominence but about embracing the profound responsibility to love and serve God and His people. It's about the weight of guiding souls, shepherding hearts, and being accountable for spiritual growth. It's about willingly accepting the mantle of leadership and enduring through both the joys and the challenges that lie ahead.

September 20, 2020, marked the culmination of a journey but also the beginning of a new chapter—one where my calling was set in stone, and I committed my heart to a life of service. The global pandemic may have altered plans, but it could not alter the divine call placed upon my life. On that unforgettable day, I stepped into the role of a minister, unshaken by circumstances and unwavering in my commitment to love, serve, and shepherd with all my heart, soul, mind, and strength.

Chapter 25

The Convergence of Life, Family, and Ministry: Embracing the Present Reality

In the ever-turning pages of life's story, I find myself in a place of remarkable convergence—a point where family, ministry, and calling have woven together into a beautiful tapestry that speaks of God's faithfulness and divine orchestration. As I stand in the present reality, I am awestruck by how every twist, turn, and challenge has led me to this moment.

The spring of 2021 marked the culmination of a transformative journey as I graduated from Southeastern University with a Master of Arts in Ministerial Leadership. Even though education was not the pinnacle—but a steppingstone and launching pad for what lay ahead—the depth of knowledge and insight gained during those years of study has enriched my ministry, equipping me to serve with greater wisdom and discernment.

In spring 2022, Melissa and I received an unexpected invitation—one that would propel us into a new phase of ministry. Our senior pastor entrusted us with the leadership of a team tasked with planting a new church campus in the city of West Boca, Florida. The prospect was both exhilarating and humbling, a reminder that God's plans often exceed our own. With the weight of this opportunity resting upon my shoulders, we embarked on a journey of preparation, prayer, and strategic planning.

In May of 2023, a new chapter began as Melissa and I assumed the role of campus pastors over West Boca. The task of shepherding a growing community and nurturing spiritual growth now rests in our hands. Our calling has become clearer than ever—the opportunity to lead, guide, and impact lives for the sake of the Kingdom. Every experience, every challenge, and every moment of growth has uniquely equipped us for this role.

June 2023 marked another significant milestone as I celebrated a decade of service on staff with Christian Life Center—a decade of growth, challenges, victories, and deepened relationships. Looking back, I am reminded of the divine setup that led me to this point—the miraculous moments, the divine appointments, and the unwavering faith that carried me through. Each step, whether triumphant or trying, has been an essential part of the journey.

The divine setup that began with a desperate cry for help has transformed into a life marked by purpose, passion, and service.

As I reflect on the passage of time, I am both humbled and amazed by the transformation that has taken place within my family. My children—Devin, Grace, and Noah—are now in their teenage years, each following their unique paths of growth and discovery. Devin's pursuit of higher education is a testament to his determination and potential. Grace's entry into high school marks the beginning of a new chapter filled with opportunities for learning and self-discovery. Noah's journey as a student and an athlete continues to unfold, revealing the potential within him.

My wife, Melissa, has been my steadfast partner throughout this journey. Our love and commitment have weathered storms and celebrated triumphs, a testament to the grace that sustains us. This

December, we will celebrate sixteen years of marriage—a journey marked by growth, mutual support, and the unbreakable bond of love.

As I stand in this present reality, I see the threads of God's providence woven through the fabric of my life. His faithfulness has carried me through seasons of uncertainty and moments of triumph. The divine setup that began with a desperate cry for help has transformed into a life marked by purpose, passion, and service. Looking ahead, I am filled with a sense of anticipation—knowing that the story is far from over, that the pages of life will continue to turn, revealing new chapters of divine setup and purposeful calling.

Chapter 25

Conclusion: The Divine Setup

As I reflect on the incredible journey that has led me to this point, I am in awe of the way the divine setup has unfolded in my life. It stands as a story of redemption, restoration, and the unrelenting love of a Higher Power who saw beyond my mistakes and weaknesses. My path has been marked by divine appointments, orchestrated by a force greater than my own understanding.

Throughout this journey, I have learned that no matter how lost we may feel, there is always hope. Even in our darkest moments, God's hand is at work, guiding us toward a purpose we may not fully comprehend. It's a purpose rooted in grace, forgiveness, and the transformative power of love.

As I've embraced my own divine setup, I've come to realize that the greatest gift of all is the gospel of Jesus Christ. In Him, I have found forgiveness for my past mistakes, a fresh start, and the promise of eternal life. Jesus, the ultimate expression of God's love, came to bridge the gap between humanity's brokenness and divine perfection.

If you are reading this and have felt the weight of your own mistakes, know that you're not alone. *The divine setup* is for all of us, no matter where we've been or what we've done. It's an invitation to experience the transformational power of grace and to step into a life filled with purpose and hope.

The gospel is simple: God loves us, despite our flaws, and He offers us a way to be reconciled to Him through Jesus. It's a free gift, waiting for you to accept it.

If you're ready to experience the joy and freedom that comes from surrendering your life to Jesus, I invite you to pray this prayer with me:

> Dear Heavenly Father, I come before you just as I am, with all my faults and shortcomings. I acknowledge that I need your forgiveness and your love. I believe that Jesus died for my sins and rose again, offering me new life. I invite Jesus into my heart and commit to following Him. Thank you for your grace and your presence in my life. In Jesus's name, Amen.

If you've prayed this prayer, welcome to the family of believers! Your journey has just begun, and I encourage you to find a community of faith to support you as you walk this path. Remember, the divine setup is ongoing, and with God by your side, your story is just beginning.

About the Author

Born and raised in the vibrant yet challenging streets of Detroit, Shawn Kelly O'Neill's life story is a powerful witness to the transformative power of faith in God, resilience, and unwavering determination. Shawn's journey from a troubled youth to a dedicated family man and ordained minister is a source of inspiration to many.

Shawn's early years were marked by adversity and hardship, as he navigated the complexities of a challenging environment. It was during these tumultuous times that he found peace and redemption in a place few would expect—prison. Behind those formidable walls, Shawn discovered a deep and abiding connection with God that would shape the course of his life.

After his spiritual awakening, Shawn embarked on a path of self-discovery and personal growth. He dedicated himself to his faith, determined to turn his life around and make a positive impact on the world. His commitment to transformation led him to pursue theological studies and ultimately become an ordained minister in the Assemblies of God.

Shawn's educational journey was further enriched by his pursuit of an Executive Master of Arts in Leadership, which equipped him with the knowledge and skills necessary to lead with compassion and purpose. This educational foundation has been instrumental in his role as a pastor and community leader.

As Campus Pastor at Christian Life Center in Fort Lauderdale, Florida, Shawn has played a pivotal role in shepherding his congregation on their spiritual journeys. His dynamic leadership, heartfelt messages, and unwavering dedication have inspired many to deepen their faith and actively participate in the life of the church.

Shawn's passion for spreading the message of hope extends beyond the church walls. He is known as a "movement catalyst" and church planter, actively involved in establishing new churches and revitalizing existing ones, bringing hope and spiritual guidance to diverse communities.

In addition to his role as a pastor and church planter, Shawn is also recognized as an evangelist and prison minister. His tireless efforts to share the message of redemption and transformation have touched the lives of countless individuals, offering them hope and a path to spiritual renewal.

Beyond his ministry, Shawn has a diverse range of passions that bring balance to his life. He is an enthusiastic pickleball player, finding joy and camaraderie on the court. His love for the culinary arts allows him to explore flavors and cuisines, creating memorable experiences for his family and friends.

One of Shawn's most cherished pursuits is mentoring young men, guiding them on their journey to becoming responsible, compassionate, and spiritually grounded individuals. His dedication to mentorship reflects his belief in the power of positive role models to shape future leaders.

Shawn's greatest source of pride and joy is his family. He is married to Melissa O'Neill, and together they are the loving parents of three wonderful children: Devin, Grace, and Noah. Melissa's unwavering support has been a cornerstone of Shawn's journey, and their family bond is a tribute to their shared values and love for one another.

Shawn Kelly O'Neill's life story is a testimony to the transformative power of faith, perseverance, and the unwavering belief in the possibility of redemption. His journey from a troubled past to a life dedicated to spreading hope and faith serves as an inspiration to all who hear his story.

Shawn continues to inspire and lead, leaving a legacy of faith, service, and the enduring power of personal transformation for generations to come.

www.ingramcontent.com/pod-product-compliance
Ingram Content Group UK Ltd.
Pitfield, Milton Keynes, MK11 3LW, UK
UKHW021919190726
13853UKWH00002B/741